Peacocks

Peacocks

*The glisten of the Peacocks
may shine …*

Illusory Poems #1

CIARAN PERKS

THE CHOIR PRESS

First published in the United Kingdom in 2020 by
The Choir Press

ISBN 978-1-78963-149-4

Contents

Perception

Prancing around the illusion of life,
Enter, thoughts of limitless mystery,
Rage, fury, bitterness, strife,
Creation of man, and his history,
Encapsulate the thoughts of the stranger.
Pathetic are the cries of the youth,
Tension, like clouds, only dense with malice,
Intent on routine, yet without balance.
On an intertwined soul,
Numbed with a meek weeping, and an aura of disgrace.

A Day in Nature

Hands glide in ponds
the enchanting sighs of the leaves
that were bronze
escape the reality in response
to a heavy sole.
And the steel grass repellent
of chlorophyll
bleeds green.

The Growth

Cobbled destinations characterised
with stressed incisions
stood before her loving shadow.
His mistress called from but a
different angle
as to not disturb or interrupt,
but to interpret a newer perspective.

The choreography of the
organic growth,
only a purpose of intrigue,
in a highlighted tint of
turquoise,
slipped through the streets.

Oxygenated

Talking, in knotted streams,
ores of crystalline roses
betraying the soil from which
they were born.

A body of thick pine,
dancing in subtlety against
the oxygenated grasp of the
atmosphere.
Wings of the avocado hues
darken the solidified pores
with a dampened wit.

The water, laced with sleeves
of gold,
enchanting, was its evergreen
essence.
Unwritten, the passages and
thoughts of the unwilling,
pacing around a candle-lit
fortune.

Realisation

In tears and trembles does
the realisation occur,
yet through the pleasure
an event of unwilling desire
pursues.

Strangled by questions
which beckon insight,
the indentations of the
fortified hourglass
glisten with each passing
whisper.

Almighty

In confused strands,
painful thorns,
a crown of such,
and in the light of his hands.

In curves,
facets,
and in shape,
and in rapids which were spat
on by limestone.

In dreams, fruit,
construction and time,
all have been served with an end.

Her

Acting in innocence,
bolts of silk and leather,
engraved by her comforting skin,
push through;
through harm, not through
ease.

Her magnified dignity had
concealed her uncut glory.
The petals of silk decorating
her laces fell with such
glory.

And, though such thoughts were
not fully conceived,
perched in persistence, she
lays down in acknowledgement.

A Previous Rain

A previous rain
created a glossy slate.
With sugar-laced rays
skimming their tones in
synchronisation, a slate's
anxiety was unlocked.

In the atmosphere of decay,
iron grooves clenched in fists
without concern,
uniform in secrecy.
What slept beneath the
slate's anxious society
saw only a constructed light,
reflected from the previous rain.

The Fallen

In spite, only the rain fell.
In resistance, only the bricks fell.
In satisfaction, only the tears fell.

Why write? It had already been
written.
Why cry? Those tears had fallen
before.
Why go? The footsteps wouldn't have been
new.
Why? But only in life.

Is it so? Your respectful despise lingers
through experiences?
Is it so? You continue to question
your answers?
Is it so? Separation is the derivative of
your will?
When you soon fall,
questioning means sorrow.

I have fallen,
like the neon petals
of your night lamp.
And,
the repetitive copying
of prior times may
continue, for they have
not fallen.

Breathe

Curtailed avenues inspired ignorance.
Laid on the quaking solids
were beings of chlorinated lungs.

With tar intertwining their
ornate breathing patterns,
and fumes complimenting their
nicotine-dosed disposition,
they faced lashes thicker
than a slave's lacerations.

Hung from a thread of warmth,
and a slight hint of comfort,
swung inconsolable silhouettes.

Pages

Hitchhiking across valleys of pine
was a depiction, scratched.
Torn clods enriched ideas,
bound by cotton.
Atomic points drowned,
and the charcoal solution
dried.

Another One

I provided sweet nothings
through a honey-glazed lisp,
and a rose-tinted vision.

You growled in a subtle speech,
black in colour,
and sour in taste,
and bitter, like that
salt-infused tear which strolled
from the exit of your
crocodile eyes.

It exiled in your lying passion
of guilt,
for you had none.

No More Time

In sixty-one seconds
and a birch exterior,
fell a sewn desire.
A tree of knowledge,
engravings of a short-lived love,
and an over-exaggerated influence
of the ruby gemstone.

Heightened in pitch,
and an energetic tempo,
like if they were a guitar,
I would select the next one,
which was made from pine.

Controlling

Place me there.
Quickly, only in precision.
Engrave my name.
Carve it in your limestone.
I'll watch you.
Over, from where you left
me.
You left me.
And carved into me.
And ran away.
In a conversation, the only participants
were you and yourself.

Addressed to Whoever

Your face may have
changed.
Your features, they contrast
from a time
before.
My words have become loose
with my thoughts.
Stretched and,
what appears,
an amalgamation
of a repetitive feeling.

Blurry

As I scribe unnecessarily into
the next date–
it will
haunt;
only coming from the metaphorical
body is a maelstrom of ideas
and hyperactive realities.
I find myself desiring,
but I haven't found Myself.
Only other beings, entities of
entertainment – only passing my
line of time, like an engraving
in ice.
The engravings fade
into a pool of memories.

Fragmented Times

These written splashes
of fragmented times.
All constructed from embarrassed
electrical experiences, and of the
fondness and approval of the
conscious memories.

Narrating the attack of the
confused includes the
eternal, but never certain
embodiment which commands
an admiration of other
embodiments.

What will pursue, through
all judgements made, will
continue to be splashes of
fragmented times.

Sensible

I'll pick it back up
after a subtle delay of
blindness.
It shall be carried through
polished shades of indigo
and crimson.
Now we can't see.

But this filter of perception
never admits defeat,
and crafts its ideas once
enabled through sense.

Actual

Rapidly turning in twirling
grooves includes spasms of
the recognition of a muse.
He was powered by desire,
and greeted with a deluded
possibility.

Developing relations strengthen
with experiences, and
unnecessary statements disease the
delusion.

Another pulse of recognition
inspires a critical dosage
of actuality, tasting
a realising regret.

Understanding Rarely Realises Acceptance

Understanding rarely realises
acceptance.
However, it is hidden in the
angularity of the multifaceted
differences, in which two
of the same written
passages cannot change
to identify with each other.
Statements are coming
to fruition through unchanged
words. Interpretations of
interrelated thought
change stripped meaning.

Acknowledgement and Will Power

The routine
of Acknowledgement
and its partner; Will Power.

They only left home once
they agreed on the current circumstances.
In their frustration, they denied
to exist, as they knew it
wasn't beneficial.

Their house, black-coated
and facts bloated in a delusional
disarray.
They were true, but only
to the acknowledging,
and its powerful will.

Collisions

The collisions of loud waves
are interpreted.
The collision of an organ
which reveals memory through
its folds should be a model of insight.
The decorated habitat is
welcome to all, and home to
one.
With collisions, inspiration cannot
occur.

Sunfish

Inscriptions of paint
smothered on a wall,
decryptions of code
told to all.
Unlike the molten
wax,
asleep with its limbs, praying,
the Sunfish in the grass drowns
with the daisies and the tulips.

And, what with concrete secretions
and creatures creasing like a fountain
of paper,
so fond of the tiring gale of
the screaming fruits,
with wheat displaying the hues
of the umber timber, stained to
satisfy.

The piping cauldron laughs with
her feathers and pentacles,
drawn to attract,
she always fails.

Blame Circumstance

So, the frightening feeling never delayed
one of passion onto another.
Reciprocation was the desired process,
and longing to hear the muttered
message.
That was him; he who caused the
unbeknownst repetition.
Only through the hint of
action does the other form
of consciousness create a
mutual understanding.
The scene, impossible in nature,
oxymoronic in events; he never
understood at this time.
Although, he did, his interpreted view
was explicitly implicit.

Like a tree, from which its origins
outdistanced the elements it was born
from, although this was a feeling.
Concealed through an acrylic liking,
where the potential was obviously
covered; the knowledge was to be
taken.
The explicated acknowledgement
tested similarity, and events held
a lack of insight, induced anticipation.
From the start, the birth, only
potential stood but excitement slept.
Now, the circumstances were as
absurd as a pond frozen over in
the summer months, or an
emerald-tinted sky.
The vocal passages then froze the
heated body, through rays
of lime.
All that stood now was a prior
disappointment, and a tree's rings
exposed.

Lonesome Visage

Only lonesome sounds had to be listened,
when the hour which changed the sky
introduced a senseless, emotional
deprivation.
The hinges, locked and rusted.
The paint, watch for its moisture.
Sounds of moths, the summer's electricity,
and a mellow dream,
did they only think.
Not only was it the killing sight which
entered with a boastful revenge.
So did our last conversation,
Saturated in a lust for a repetitive smiling.

Time, like the sandstone windowsill,
an inch of comfort, and milliseconds
of reality, held through walls of
commands.
Not only had the moths now moved,
entitled sleep never delayed
vanity.
Enter the well-known and heir to the
raggedy throne, Princess of the Penman.

She awakened the inspirational words
of the night, but–

Everybody had to sleep.
Never were these words heard,
don't say they weren't, because
somebody may have heard but
never listened.

The meaning was of ignorance,
the denial is unnecessary,
exemplified incorrectly, I must admit.
The echoes of an exhausted mind
promoted issues, such as the ones
blowing from your chimney.
In which, the smoke, like steam,
poisoned and dry however,
it replaced your once happier
sighs.
It was unfortunate how the
cause was never executed, foreseen
through the lonesome visage.

The Sorrowful Magpie

The sorrowful magpie,
solitary, he perched himself on
a community, and yet he was
at a distance to everybody.

The sorrowful magpie,
he felt the joyous magnitudes
of happiness through his
doubled greetings, however was
mellow in his singularity.

The sorrowful magpie,
he felt a spiteful despise
to those grouped without
himself.

The sorrowful magpie,
in rejection, his sorrow
gave him
comfort.

Past, Present, and Future

There is something,
residing in this experience.
Darkening this feigned, illusory script
with a spitting spite and a pain,
tight.
It should come out in the eventual
plan,
when one's own experiences limit to
enable a personal one.
They shall feel a crushing like
the personal one's; one is through
tears while the other lacks,
twining their delusion of love
through each conversational interval.

This desirable too;
one of longing,
need,
passion,
goes unnoticed in terms of
oblivious perception.
The grey strips of nothingness
do reveal a hiding factor; one
of knowledge between a
participant's duet,
found in a tripod of balance.

The times have
changed.

His Timely Friend

The percussion instrumental plays
the melody of your heart.
Stopping and starting like
an indecisive bird; stopping by for
a galactic questioning.
Stopping for his time, starting, again,
a thought once thought of before.

This bird throws its feathered ligaments
out into the pink horizon,
nerve endings enticed with the warm
particles.
An attraction,
thickened
with a loving for a timely friend.

Ever so recent was his introduction.
However, the games progressed
their fondness through differing
increments.
Maybe parallel, and they both hadn't a clue.
Their melodies played at the singular time;
Was this so rare, though?

The percussion instrumental paces through a
false warping,
With factual history denoting a future choice
to be made.
After his rest, the new thought of ruin
awakened our bird,
A possibility that this relation might lead to an
irate hate.

This relation is a collation of loving,
one who he, the timely friend,
isn't so aware of.
The bird, through a gale of curiosity,
chest upward, shoulders following,
jumped through the article which detailed the
reciprocation.

Or lack of.
The bird hadn't read the result
of these resolute inscriptions.
So he left in an unbeknownst tranquillity,
pondering his love for he, his timely friend.

The percussion instrumental continues.
It may show exhaustion and fatigue,
but never once beats late.
The perfected depression of the
bird's tiresome flap
trembled through repetition.
He almost relapsed,
in terms of his promising judgement
and,
had not heard from his timely friend.

The friend, he was busy.
Sustained features, set in ways,
a fish hunting from the surface waves.
It was comparable to a duet of
dancing snails,
with sighs for wind to fly their sails.
Like a penguin learning to climb,
an entitled pig dining on limes,
a cross-hatched melody full of rhythm,
and displaced time.

The percussion instrumental,
such an interval.
It was laid with mortar,
and poor placements of a brittle
chestnut.

Our bird, feathers inverted, talons
outstretched, disposition introverted,
flew to the Crayon Canyons.
Busting body, flustered mind,
blushing cheeks, a pain-induced cry.
Also, he landed in a striped engagement.

An experience of years, arrived,
and fruit, still alive.
The only tree for miles,
named properly, 'the Cactus.'
But the bird, for his loving,
like a set of scales, outweighed
hate, causing debate.

The thoughts of him, so oblivious,
inspired his companion, our bird,
to traverse the universe
in search for his timely
friend.

The percussion instrumental,
he remembered as he aged.
Like a comb through the hair
of a dictator,
He entertained the musical passage.
On the roots of the buttered granary,
he fed.
The bird mingled in a seeded
crying, and printed the act thrice.

The timely friend had spoken.
In rapid fractals of sun-burning rattles,
and misleading notifications
causing his battles,
the bird, scratched palms, feeling calm,
ran through the reverent
firmament with a deep excitement.

The percussion instrumental,
ending in a pace so slow,
one with an opalescent despondency
to be viewed at a show.
The friend greeted our now
transcendent predator with a sigh so
uncaring,
as if to say I wouldn't care if you
were rotting in the ground,
blaring.

The bird offered conversation,
topping the fuel tank up with an
overspill of naivety.
He had driven his creation,
in shambles and repairs,
to this act of reckoning.
It was only a night ago
they danced in a fortuitous
gratitude for their prior greeting.
The percussion,
in their dual minds,
caused pounding vibrations
at the soles of their clawed feet.

The bird's heart,
heating and beating, witnessed the
sombre apology, apathetic but confused.
Deluded sadness was the illness
diffused over each monochromatic
feather held in his unknowing
realisation.
Was it he who played the percussion?

The timely friend split from partnership,
hence the hindering of his midnight
passion.
The misery, content in its
placement of its home,
carefully placed, in fact, on the
estate of the friend's speech.

The percussion instrumental,
its loving weighing nigh on two tons,
its hating on three.
Regret was the one thing
a placed bet could win.
The bird offered his wing
and sought after a loving,
or a response to his
illegible thinking.

He lit his candles,
retained his cactus rashes,
grabbed the jade handles
of the urn supplying a home for his
ashes.

They spread in the bitter frost of the
canyon's breath,
and that article he once read,
it had been published.
His timely friend reciprocated.

My Loving

My loving.
In rarity and in unexpected dates
does this feeling occur.
One bound by a rose velvet, stitched
through polyester experiences.
The recipient would either
wear this scarf of admiration,
or carefully return to the
original creator.
Something will tell you my
current love.
I wear it, the scarf, rose-tinted,
and stitched with polyester,
Unwilling to gift to even the
most willing.
That day has come, although
the return of my scarf has
inspired me to take care of it.
The bearer couldn't hold it,
for the timing was not correct,
but I know it is still in his
sentimental possession.
My keen aquamarine eyes
may find a similar day, though.

Your loving,
comes through a want to
associate.
With serpentine scales
and screaming fails.
Your loving
comes through desire.
Like a spire of a cold coal fire,
and intelligent crafts to disrupt
positivity.

Like a nativity,
only for the dismantled happiness.
And this one has no right
to feel a hating spite.
A nativity for a death.
Common sense,
ignored her breath,
the persuasion of
your loving.
Collapsed,
once stood tall, yes, naive,
but an aptitude for strength.
And only a present
debris flew through the wind
of sense.
Your loving,
haunting with flaunting facets
of seemingly daunting lights,
one making another tremble
with a false conclusion.

Again, the complete
and ever so whole
feeling of the malicious
hatred I periodically feel
for loving has arrived.
It will, and already has
reached a boredom,
where the things that lack
become my target for
the familiar anger I
possess.
I know that the reason
the common association of
all red hues can resemble
adoration and frustration,
an explanation of the selected
crimson tones my scarf
reflects.

The aching hour
of the effervescent feeling.
For it will never pass,
only return.
Returned to its
sender.
I have aged in a week,
for my thoughts are minutes,
and these minutes occur every
second, every
breath.
Lingering to death,
my life's trade shall be
longing

for a thing to be
returned to its
sender.
And I can only think of
you,
for you shall ignore my
calling.
I have rolled the dice,
A six rolled in threes, how nice.
An underwater chiming,
ringing like the alarm
of the day you wake up
to go to your father's
Funeral.
And the rain, drowning
the times our ink-written
escapades took place.
So I hand this burden
to nature, and it
shall be returned to
its
sender.
A whistle,
the twilight's
split,
impossible,
like a solar eclipse
visible at midnight.
My edges,
tattered and ragged,
like the jutting promontory
crafted from the tools of my
chest,

Fly in the
buzzing shades
of the song of a
warbler.
I painted the gift
in a sarcastic
gold,
once in a polyester rose,
now in a false alloy
of spite and despise.
My loving,
in a harsh brilliance
and a brazen resurrection,
deafens and fades
in spasms of
white noise.
My loving,
putting coal, the heat
admirer,
through a wet, cooler
spitting;
pulls you in for a
taped conversation.
It sticks so rough,
and when reviewed in a
newer mood,
I lose balance
through disgust.
This lucid hesitation,
using a typeface of despair,
a bubble of acid,
and a life in need of
repair,

maintains the strict
organisation of the
aching pain.
Aching, this is the partner,
the married participant in
the loving of a trinity.
The holy pain,
and the unholy longing,
in a cauldron of crying may
reveal
my loving.

I Feel

I
can feel,
I
will feel,
depriving of a
youthful containment.
In his partnership,
new beginnings cease,
growing will not occur.
And
brightened eyes illuminate
in and out of this
righteous forest,
timing impeccable,
heated with a blaze of
jealousy.

What Are You Thinking?

Take me up into the sky,
up, so high, into your eyes,
your spacecraft illuminates
the chamber, the soul
of me.

Abduct my regret, for it
stings and lingers.
Abduct my loving, for it holds
a weary impatience.
Abduct my mind, for I am only
searching for vengeance.

He, however, will choose to stay,
speaking a cryptic language
called reality.
He shall live here indefinitely,
move across the oceanic,
diaphanous manta rays,
with a partner, and find a
reef for a home.

Take me up, into the sky,
up, so high, into your eyes,
your spacecraft
Illuminates the chambers,
the core, the soul
of me.

My repetitive ways cannot
comprehend a break in
the way other people thrive.
I analyse, study, and ponder
the depths of the sky.

In multifaceted, feathered paint,
plastered upon a wall of lies,
a molecular impulse of
an ecstatic energy
poisons me, and brings a
liquified sorrow to my eyes.

He is I and I am Him

As he sat writing his path,
I studied his face.
What I saw included a
desire for the past.
He longed for an experience
which happened years before,
but always questions the
unchanging reality.
There were cobbles, maintained
for their strength,
their visual qualities
putrefied.
He would analyse the fact
that nobody had criticised
vision,
so he noted it.
Beings wrongfully acting, but
he asked me the question,
Who is to say they are wrong?

He holds a great admiration
for a new relation.
The person in question,
he'd be a new revelation
to the boy, writing.
He blames the circumstances,
and their timing,
and despises all who dares
question him.
For me, I think he feels
he questions himself too
much for others to do so.
May that be bad, or wrong,
let one decipher.
The only revealed piece,
is that he is I and I am
him.

Stop Abiding

I am not supposed to rhyme,
but this time,
I shall.
Let's break conventions,
make new inventions.
Stop abiding by the citizens'
opinion.

What else do they love?
Patterns.
It is basic, makes life a tad
easier, organisation is key
to efficiency.

Let's imagine I
whisper these words,
addressed to the silent-
type.
Unsuccessful,
and utterly useless
are these planted words.

Some will take an
amazement,
I am colder.
Some will adjust their opinion
to my liking,
just speak.

I'm now exhaling at, well,
an unidentifiable amount.
It's to the reader, and
their view.

How would you see me?
Ignorant, arrogant, insecure?
A sheep to the rules,
a maverick to confusion,
I will stop abiding.

The Ballad of Mr. Beetle

The beetle shall reach a
refreshment period through edible
cellular emeralds.
Glistening through dew, his trap
creates satisfactory sounds.
Audible satisfaction, the
several-sighted specimen
labels his crunch.

Like a brunch for an elder
couple living on the outskirts
of a foreign land,
sharing sexuality through
golden cutlery,
oriental-patterned handkerchiefs
in hand.

Stabbing swathes of plant life
and clods decorated the
beetle's mind.
His territorial, almost
leather-textured pads walked
the land like a strutting cat.

This cat was a vain stray,
absorbed in an ironically
materialistic view of itself,
unaware it is no better
than an impoverished rat
dining on an acrylic bulb.

The beetle, as beautiful as his
humanoid counterparts
explained, grew greedy and
pitiful.

He longed for others to
create donations,
excuses were made so his
tiny life would be satisfied.
The next point of order,
Mr. Beetle;
an unimportant deity
he held the comparison to.

The beetle climbed the
capitalism tree,
held together by financial crises,
starving men in their
mid-nineties,
and the king of the tree
who built a castle of
honey-glazed hexagons atop
the capitalistic hills.

Now, it was a queen instead.
Mrs. Bee, infamous for
smoothly removing the life of
her son's wife.
He, the beetle, knew she didn't
die under the knife,
and so, full of strife, Mrs. Bee
stated it was really something
to do with her vocal
Mannerisms.

The beetle had made it to
the confrontation of
Mrs. Bee.

Then the beetle woke.
In a date, so bespoke
to himself.
He found the society of grass
he once floundered around,
he was welcome, but a black
sorrow filled his hexagonal eyes.

He understood what it was like
to be stripped of everything.
In this newfound communal trust,
the beetle reached a new
refreshment period.

My Truth

I've opened my truth up to
myself,
Like a bookend collecting its
words on a shelf,
selfless and solitary,
crafted from a willow who
weeped his rhymes for the
last time.

I've demonstrated my truth to
myself,
found from a sea-thriver's
maze of a shell,
coated with a blood thick
of the toxicity
of hell.

I've gifted my truth unto
myself,
a glorified honour lined
in steel.
It slashes the man of the
diamond heels,
and only,
the cause was the sense
to feel.

The only thing my truth has for
me,
a ravaging rupture and a raging
finale,
one forcing my eyes to
see.
It confused and bewildered me,
painfully.

The Telling Window

The curtain,
hung from lace,
ran its race,
felt displaced,
and suffocated.

The telling window,
one the gust could blow,
one pain could glow,
and let the night show.

Its 'sill,
one with will,
taken like a pill,
enabling you to be tranquil.

The telling window,
one the gust could blow,
one pain could glow,
and change my heart's tempo.

Now the wall,
straightened, unlike a ball,
witnessed the day us all
had to fall.

The telling window,
one the gust could blow,
one pain could glow,
and reveal my anguish, very slow.

His glass.
It reveals his identity, at last.
Open to interpret, opinions fast.
Telling you, you are his spell to be
cast.

The telling window,
no longer told.
He grew old,
shattered his lonesome gust.
His pain died when
the night resorted to lust,
so, he told no more.

Blue Guitar

Pinned to a mind,
shake it violently, make it
hard to find.
Spun from black webs,
hold my glowing hand until
it flows and ebbs.

Cracking the glass,
magnifying glory shining
through.
Hung from lace,
I can't keep on going,
will not win the race.

Swimming in a conscious
state of ice-like tar,
and all you are doing is sitting
there, playing your
blue guitar.
I do not know the answer to
how to raise the bar,
cherry red roses were
painted on your
blue guitar.

I am not one,
there are parts never to
be shown.
All on my own,
petty lies not willing to
compromise.

Screeching from the halls,
barbaric metal cages
and heightened walls.
I cannot see,
I am blinded by dignity.

Running through the conscious
thoughts of a liar,
and all I do is sit there
listening to your
blue guitar.
Glazed in a brazen
attack of a crystalline water,
acrylic tulips grew faintly on
your
blue guitar.

Branded on my mind,
I shook it violently,
made it hard to find.
I spun it from my
wool,
made you think I was a glass
half-full.

Shattered fortune.
I was lost in my garden
of lullabies and tunes.
Hung from a thread,
I watched, you kept on
going,
now you're dead.

Bound to a world where
I can be alone.
That wasn't true however,
I was forced to hear the cries
of your
blue guitar.
Your exposed tendons
played tensed melodies from
afar,
but that was when I wanted
to listen to your
blue guitar.

Singular

I scratch and
I scream.

The hassle,
what you have named,
plays,
and your actions,
all on my mind.

Mourning Spider

I can visualise the
end.
It is
a conscious dwelling.
Squat and concrete,
and seventeen
ligaments
hanging like
suicides.
Smoking lungs,
and breathing cigars.
These sticks
painted iodine blots
on skin-toned clots.

To you,
for when I am walking,
a confusion of
mindful ignorance.
Challenging inference,
and
smothered in a crosshatched
watercolour humming,
and legs,
the eight strips
with the content belonging
of the
mourning spider.

Am

I am writing,
for I
am
writing nothing.
I am feeling for
I
am
feeling nothing.
My pacing gasp,
for a strong longing,
it waits for one,
loving none.

Close, Far

Close,
once.
They drank salvaged tastes,
making haste
for conversation.
He sat up from a distant slumber,
and a subtracting thought
to ask
of their recent happenings.

They replied,
quick to insult.
It was not one to amuse,
and so
changed course.

How,
building bricks daily,
swimming in frustrated currents
and overwhelmed speech;
it is exhausting,
maintaining an illusion-dressed
peace,
especially in its act of
destruction.

Ill,
cyanide and acidic juice,
the diluted death of
now, so
far.

Bundles

I,
the paint is wet,
the pain, watery. My,
eyes are torn,
tears, blue grass
and frogs with eight legs.
Heptagonal, fattened
worlds, slow and lazy.
I heard those words,
flows and flowers
Rosemary and time,
to go.
I know.
Quickened spite.
Heating music.
Train knocking pace
with no space to
galaxy.
For
I
can't
cut my hair, will you.
Shaven sheep and money on the desk.
Axe and chains
hang in his
softer skin,
and sliced
arteries.

For You, Pollyanna

For your happiness,
like an island with
rose and lilac shoes,
floral curlicues
and a hatred for the misused.
One to amuse,
in a pitch of the highest,
most sought-after
green.
Gorgeous, more than one
can see.
And your name,
a reflection of
those who are
happy.

Isn't Life Beautiful?

Such a disgrace,
not up to par.
These continental quakes,
through fire, and
the collisions of galactic
elements,
they were fascinating,
obviously.
Because, life is beautiful,
almost,
in fact,
it holds a runners-up
prize to
death.

It Isn't For You

The connection was forced
into standard.
It was dry and
it had embraced a
lying.

For I couldn't recognise
how much care I
didn't have for loving or
life.

Not reserved
specifically through
my view of
you,
so don't feel
unique.

Defenestration, But of Thoughts

How fast to act,
it is quick for opinion
like an assumption of the
ever-lost past.

So I grabbed the frame,
screwed in by overs.
Well, I had the frame.
The frame was my mind.

Caught, you had me,
like dusk robins in a
hollow decadence.
For mortality,
but the crack of
the lungs lingered.

I filed its tears–
Remember! Always file in
the direction of the grain.
So the words hit
my heart,
not my spine.

My fortune, or ill-omened
future,
it hung like a dousing
pendulum.

And I laugh
as I desire it to tell me
good,
but it was made of
pyrite.

Peacocks

His turquoise edges have
been sliced through a glimpse of a
histrionic light.
They stand through a vibrating
lust, opposing its strict disposition.
And what does he do other
than strengthen his million-eyed
gaze?
An intensified delusion.
One of passionate interrelations.
He experiences his literary
contemplations through faceted
reflections, blinding all but
the bird.
A tile pool, paused hues, diced
through a precise grinding.
Drenched in an ocean of opulence,
the bird places his topaz
talons into the natural
oasis.

How his hues have changed,
from turquoise irises to indigo
indentations.
A command from the council
of the red hue,
two partners share both loving
and an instinct of revolt through
an equidistant split of matter.
Crimson and Cadmium,
they were named.
They eliminate their opposition,
all that was green,
and fuse through blue's
primary light.
What was left was a revealing
bouquet of feathered hinges,
coruscations of hydration and
satisfaction.
There was only one thing that
had yet to take its role in time.
It had contained the heart.

Stepping from the illuminated
gallons.
A liquified boast of
magenta, through the thinnest of
strands.
And, without hands,
but a spine of experimentation
and sensuality stood like
a beacon of a romanticised hope.
For he was simply a creature,
another of the trillions, however
he was a watcher.
Thriving on foresight,
one could not say
this tropical deity possessed
anything else but beauty.
His craft, one of travel,
decorated in systematic
directions of palm and
steel leaves, had
took off one last time.

An era, at an end.
And only in his mind to mend,
like a kite flying high in
the mires of the Underworld,
or a liquified loving diced
to an emulsion with the
ocean of distaste.
He turned and faced us all,
in charm, he stood too tall.

Each groove of his
oil-painted being pierced the
pandemonium of the damned.
The only visualisation we can
be deserving of includes
description.
as bare sight becomes
glass so thin it shatters in the
wind.

Finally, the incense of
those blue-heart tulips
enchanted the
golden-appendaged beast.
Fine charcoal rinsed and
whitened the squat jaw
he possessed,
one fine maw,
it was almost against the
law.
For all times come to
a blend in the tulip garden,
how, if all past times
can be read, then all futures
can be written,
in his presence.
He lined the cobble pathway
with sprouting shrubs,
a chlorophyllic claustrophobia
ignited in the flames of the
emerald and aventurine
recesses.
Bound by a newfound silver,
and a craving for the material,
the intoxicated timing of
the profound adoration
laid like slate in the construction
of the monarch's tomb;
fused into the maelstrom of
his eyes.

The tulips bloomed in the
summer, humming its tune,
and the trinity of time slept
in the garden
of peacocks.

To You, I Write For

It started through an unweighted
tapping,
like honey-drowning orbs
whispering in a shallow melody
onto my roof.
He wanted to let me know,
after recent events,
it seemed undeclared, yet very
clear-cut.
He took my hand through
truths and anger,
in melancholic rhythms,
and
embarrassment.

I commanded myself to
stay in the waiting room.
My appointment was at
half the following hour,
so there, it exposed
my early arrival.

The micro-aquarium of sorts,
tightened through oxygenated
shackles,
and a freezing, tropical
cackling.

The doctor asked to my
attendance.
For it was ill-will,
I painted my response around.
It was like asking a
tourist for directions in a
foreign land,
he hadn't an answer.
So why did he have a prescription?

I ran around already
knowing,
for my thoughts never finish,
but my realised thoughts,
verbally,
pause.

My spiteful lust,
and a natural loving,
for nothing,
got me home.
It was your message
sleeping in the gaseous
bowl.
One of flames
and a humidity,
not of a sighing liquid,
designed to decompose
instead of telling.
Yet it was a hint,
you didn't want me to
know.

Notice the changing intentions?
They stay the same,
my interpretation
differs.
Pacing,
I'll pin it to the wall.
So I took you from the
blaze,
and hung your charred
lowercase to the marriage
noose.
I knew it was hard to hint,
but when did the explicit
never reveal?

Horse-Racing Lover

I'm sat up for you,
not willing,
obviously.
Apparently,
this horse, colour-blind,
and tranquil,
under the caffeinated
illusion of the rider.

His love for you is
false.
It is,
when you fall,
your bloody systems
will crawl from the beating
of a bullet.

Mania

How I have moved
in a subtle organisation.
In thought, I read.
And, the tapered clock
turns square,
with a fear for the
aware.
Distant peaking,
in layers,
washes an indoctrinated
mind with more
specifics.

I am forever in mania,
whether a delusion satisfies
isn't so known to my
being.
And,
reminders of things,
forms,
conscious forms,
all to aggravate through
interrogation.
For a void of water droplets
entered into my
imperfect
soul,
would I ever leave
from the impure purity?

Lavender Loving

In your streak of
your curlicued fate;
from the decision of the
place your creators
chose to house you,
to the unbeknownst desire
you feel to perform
a certain
task,
we aligned.

At the moment of guessed
times,
and the moment they were
named fact.
to the choices of pressure,
and how they act.

In those black tree fringes,
to the point of when I
attached my imperishable
door on its hinges,
the perennial moment
shall live in permanence,
for that was the moment
we spoke.

The molten moral fibres
of our core had
congregated in a
swift, conjugal manner.

My betrayal,
of such conventions I
had gifted to my earlier self;
I had forborne such a
commitment.
So, I write to a new
commitment.

In the sapphire lakes of
Jupiter,
there shall be found;
gaseous shards of a tourmaline,
decorated in the shades of
the Earth's morning
frost.
For these Arctic fractals
ponder their own
perpetuity.

The hornet flies in
his content, unaware bliss,
and replicates the
springtime musical of its
cousins, the bees and the
wasps.

Found in a community
of fear-induced foresight
are worlds of dew and pollen.
In similarity, the folks
live in duality,
and quite the limit to resources,
and resourcefulness,
a lack of knowledge
to the unforeseen,
divine gathering of
three colours in a
Rock pool of
refulgent particles.
A trio of compliments
hold the names of Lilac,
Lavender and Mauve.

And, in this partnership
of Purple,
they long for repeated
experience.

Mauve travelled to
the sand-decorated dunes
across Egypt,
keeping her presence closer
to Babylon.

Lilac resided in Eden,
for the metaphorical
strips of the lucid lime
hues had complimented her
materialistic paraphernalia.

Lavender searched for
a scape of orange, in a
sunburnt longing for
rumination.
How it was found, was
through a third-eye
visualisation.

In ventilated dreaming
did our time, however,
stop.
It creased and cringed
and, once deceased,
but in another time, loved.
It admired, and breathed.

Atmospheric piano.
The familiar piece of the
keys once pressed
reminisced their time in a
form before.
For they were as conscious
as a death toll.
They also gave life through
the explication of
sound.

To hold your surface,
and to embrace your
experienced breathing,
I would only replace it
with an eternal life with
you.

Replacing your loving
for your loving, but longer.
In the mirror, after
the fact, your legs tensed
as much as your hair
curled,
hilarity arrived because
your bronze soothing
had been, admittedly,
rough, but
straight nonetheless.

You were strapped in an
electric passion,
with the fading pulsations.
My hand on yours,
my eyes in your irises.
I feel like they had shone
blue, but hazel is a
possibility.

Mauve, Lilac, and Lavender
played in a chorus,
for the impoverished.
I was, not in the
literal sense,
for feeling had been lacking.

I'm sighing in the
bed of roses,
Lilac wanted rid of them.
You told her of calm
resolutions, in her sixth-
century infancy, she
felt appeased.

Mauve warned of an end,
although, foresight couldn't
be strengthened, for she
was locked in a habit
for exploring paradigms.
Lavender had created these
paradigms, so Mauve
could be clarified.

My respect towards authority
is utterly in limit, and
you begged to replay memories.
I begged to you the same,
through the physical
exchange of my love.

It was of the last experiences,
and this purple dream returned
to the awaiting luxuries of the
afterlife.

I asked you to show me
your truth,
and like a slow murder,
or a continual branch
of copper,
this reality,
a cyclone of Australia,
or a Brazilian afternoon,
I came to wake.
In my bed of Lavender.

The Hibiscus Dream

A personal misery
dressed in mint and vanilla tattoos
and cultural abnormalities
splitting in laughs and blushing.
The pedals of the
mandala clockwork twisted
in nebulas of gravel
and charcoal.

The river of decay fulfilled
its infrared ardour through
weakening youthful ligaments
and organs, and
reducing them to a
hydrated
dying.

Shrouded are memories of unclear
disgust,
for the emphasis of rusted
age creates illusions.
The rust on metal
is like a hunger
belonging to a creature
without a mouth.
As if to deprive a being
of its ability to digest,
towards its end,
all morals are
ignored.

A blot from the cog's charcoal,
stripped into an intoxicated
overdose.
The charcoal rapidly dreams
of inscriptions cf mushrooms
and moss,
painted on the forehead of
a lapis lazuli gemstone.

Smooth, deficient in facets,
aluminium lips
belonging to a falcon
high on acid.
This acidic dream, of
heavens bound in
cattle skin,
transforms reality through
the smell of a loud gun.

Shooting the interdimensional
cardboard with the snout
of a pig,
the chimney pipes its soul
through its tri-tipped tree-tops,
and the brick-and-cement leaves
turn the sky blonde
from the bleach of the fire.

Is it so? You continue to
even question your answers?
The fortified hourglass had
now shattered from Lavender
shades.
I shall keep questioning,
for the answers are left
unanswered.
And now my
mandala clockwork,
has created
the hibiscus dream.

An eternal light and a gifted wine . . .

About the Author

Ciaran Perks is an English poet and writer of the book 'Peacocks' and writes other poems and creative pieces. Growing up and living in Plymouth, Devon, he studies English Literature, and is inspired by illusory dreams, the afterlife, and space. At 17 years of age, he is working on his next poetry collection and novel.